The King's Pudding

CHAPTER 1
CORONADO HILLS ELEMENTARY

The King made a pudding.
It was round,
it was brown,
and it smelled delicious.

The King picked up his spoon.
But the Queen shouted,
"Stop! Stop!
That pudding might be too hot!
I will taste it for you."

3

So the Queen went
nibble, nibble,
munch, munch,
and some of the pudding
was gone.

"No," said the Queen,
"it wasn't too hot."

5

The King picked up his spoon.
But the Prince shouted,
"Stop! Stop!
That pudding might be too cold!
I will taste it for you."

So the Prince went
nibble, nibble,
munch, munch,
and more of the pudding
was gone.

"No," said the Prince,
"it wasn't too cold."

The King picked up his spoon.
But the Knight shouted,
"Stop! Stop!
That pudding might be too sour!
I will taste it for you."

So the Knight went
nibble, nibble,
munch, munch,
and all of the pudding
was gone.

"No," said the Knight,
"it wasn't too sour."

"My pudding!" cried the King.

The King made another pudding.
It was round,
it was brown,
and it smelled delicious.

The King picked up his spoon.
"Stop! Stop!"
shouted the Queen
and the Prince
and the Knight.
"We will taste it for you!"

"No!" said the King,
"I will taste it myself."

And that's exactly what he did!